Let Go
or
Get Dragged

LOY B. SWEEZY, JR.

Table of Contents

1. The Meaning of Letting Go 1

2. The Forgiveness Study 5

3. Joseph's Stages of Change 11

4. Things Most People Ignore
   about Letting Go. 23

5. Laws that Govern Letting Things Go 27

6. Forgiving the Klu Klux Klan's 33

7. Demonic Decoys 45

8. Church Makes a Difference 51

9. Naaman's Acceptance 55

10. Jonah's Stages to Change 61

11. Control Yourself 81

12. Manage Your Anger 87

13. Don't Come Up Short 97

About the Author 103

1

The Meaning of Letting Go

M any people struggle with letting things go. These people often wonder why it is difficult for them to overcome or break free in certain areas. The reason is because they are still holding onto things that they should have let go years ago. When you let things go, you are casting all your worries and cares on God.

> *"Cast the whole of your care [all your anxiet-ies, all your worries, all your concerns, once and for all} on Him, for He cares for you affectionately and cares about you watch-fully." (I Peter 5:7, AMP)*

Dr. Creflo Dollar, in his teaching series on *The Hand of God*, says,

> *"Take that heavy burden, difficulty or chal-lenge, that you are carrying. The one that*

has arisen due to circumstances that has created hardship and struggles in your life and fling those worries and anxiety over onto the back and hands of the Lord. Let him carry them for you. The Lord is extremely interested in every facet of your life and is genuinely concerned about your well fare."
(DVD, Part 2)

When you let go you release quickly what is on you, off you and put it into the hands of God who is equipped, and designed to handle what you cannot handle. When I was a boy, I remember one day touching the hot stove. When my hand touched the hot burner immediately, I released my hand from the burner. I released or let go of the hot burner because the human hand is not designed to handle or bear the burning, torturing pain of the hot burner.

On the contrary, when a cooking pan is placed on the hot burner, the cooking pan has no problem with taking on the heat and the intensive pressure of the fire, because the cooking pan is specifically designed to take on the hot burner.

Jesus Christ desires that you release all of your troubles and difficulties over to him. *Casting all your cares upon him; for he careth for you. (I Peter 5:7)* Instead of going through the torture of holding on to deep-rooted issues, try letting them go by casting them on Jesus and allow Him to carry what He has been designed by God to do.

When I speak of letting go, I am referring to giving up the struggle, turning the difficult situation over to God, and getting to the point to where you are willing to release your negative issues to God. You have to come to a point to where you are ready to let go of the emotional pain and disappointments, or you will get dragged.

Notice this scripture,

> *"For the wages of sin is death; but the gift of God is eternal life through Jesus Christ our Lord." (Romans 6:23)*

The point I am conveying is that if you do not let go of your secret sins, hurt and disappointments or your evil ways, they will, according to verse 23, drive you to your grave. Sin produces death, both spiritually and physically. The Devil wants you to enjoy sin, not God. God knows that sin will produce death; therefore, if there is any sin in your life, it must be confessed and released to God.

God's desire for people is joyful life in abundance, to the full and overflowing. Satan desires that your bad habits, worries and negative hang ups consume you to the point of death, demoralizing you and making you ineffective to the point of handicapping you from all kingdom of God progression and productivity.

> *"The thief cometh not, but for to steal, and to kill, and to destroy: I am come that they might have life, and that they might have it more abundantly." (John 10:10)*

The devil wants people to concentrate on the negatives more than the positives. I often go to the YMCA to play basketball. One particular day while playing, I noticed that a friend of mine was on a team that won four games back to back.

My friend's team finally lost the fifth game. When he came over to sit down beside me, I made the comment to him, *"Man you guys did really well today, you won four games straight!"* His reply was, *"Ya, but we lost the last one, and that is what I am focused on."*

I thought, *how sad* that he could not enjoy his four victories because of losing one. Satan often works the same way; he wants people to focus all of their attention on their failures, instead of focusing on godly success. God want us to focus on our victories and not our failures; God wants us to focus on the good and not the bad. If you focus on the good, then you will have the outcome of the good.

2

The Forgiveness Study

D r. Don Colbert, in his book, *Deadly Emotions,* says,

> *"A scientific project conducted at the University of Wisconsin was simply called "The Forgiveness Study." The study demonstrated that learning to forgive may help prevent heart disease in middle-age subjects. The incidence of heart disease was higher in those who admitted they could not forgive. The risk of heart disease was much lower in those who reported an ability to forgive easily. These researchers concluded that a failure to forgive is a greater predictor of physical health problems than hostility."*
> *(P. 169)*

This research on the forgiveness study can be affirmed and accurate by examining the life of **Judas Iscariot's unforgiving attitude;** Judas was one of the 12 disciples that Jesus Christ selected to follow Him while on his earthly ministry. (Matthew 10:2-4)

Initially, when Judas started out in the ministry as a disciple I am sure he had no idea or intentions of betraying Christ for money; however, because his heart was not right with God, it was not right with money. He made a bad money decision, one of which was selling out Jesus for 30 pieces of silver.

Judas felt so bad about his betrayal until he was unwilling to forgive himself; it was not that he was unable to forgive himself, but it was that he **refused** to forgive himself. The Bible says, *"If we confess our sins, he is faithful and just to forgive our sins, and to cleanse us from all unrighteousness." (I John 1:9)* That means that God is willing, ready and able to forgive you, contingent upon the fact that you will ask Him to forgive you and then believe that He has forgiven you.

> *"I have sinned," he said, "for I have betrayed innocent blood." "What is that to us?" they replied. "That's your responsibility." So Judas threw the money into the temple and left. Then he went away and hanged himself." (Mathew 27:4-5, NIV)*

Again, Judas became so obsessed with guilt from betraying Jesus until he began to have suicidal thoughts, his suicidal thoughts became so strong that he tried to kill himself, and he acted on what he thought. Judas killed himself as an attempt to relieve the pain and guilt that was associated with his betrayal. The point is that because Judas chose not to forgive himself, his unforgiving attitude became so dark within his heart until he killed himself.

An unforgiving attitude will break you down; it will stunt and handicap you from maximizing your potential. This kind of attitude will destroy your body causing it to become dysfunctional. The thing to note about an unforgiving attitude is that you do not have to accept it. You can make the decision to forgive. You choose whether to forgive yourself and others.

The ability to forgive can be seen in the life of the apostle Peter. Like Judas, Peter sinned against Christ but **Peter forgave himself** and received restoration from God for all that he did wrong. Peter denied Christ when Jesus was arrested, Peter denied that he even knew Christ, and when confronted about his connection to the ministry of Jesus, Peter acted out with very inappropriate behavior.

When Peter was questioned about his relationship with Jesus, not only did Peter lie one time, but he lied three times, denying and disowning that he ever knew

Jesus. In fact, Peter disowned Jesus in the presence of Jesus. The Bible says,

> *"Then began he to curse and swear, saying, I know not the man and immediately the cock crew and Peter remembered the word of Jesus which said unto him, before the cock crow, thou shalt deny me thrice. And he went out and wept bitterly." (Matthew 26:74-75)*

Peter literally began both, to curse himself, and to use the Lord's name in vain. In addition, he began to use excessive profanity and inappropriate language to convince the people into the lie about him not knowing Jesus. Dr. Archibald T. Robertson, says, *"He repeated his denial with the addition of profanity to prove that he was telling the truth instead of the lie that they all knew." (P. 220)*

After the rooster crowed, Peter remembered the words of Jesus and he repented. True repentance will always make you feel better. God is not interested in beating you down; He is interested in lifting you up so that you can joyously fulfill His will for your life. Peter's weeping and asking God for forgiveness was the turning point in his life not going under. Peter's life was restored from destruction, all because he released his guilt, shame, and hurt to God.

When Judas Iscariot betrayed Jesus, he acted out of

selfishness; he refused to come to God for forgiveness. He took matters within his own hands; he became so self-absorbed and overwhelmed by his betrayal of Jesus until he just could not overcome the negative thoughts of what he had done, but rather chose to kill himself.

Notice this scripture:

> *Come to me all you who labor and are heavy-laden and overburdened and I will cause you rest. [I will ease and relieve and refresh your souls.] Take My yoke upon you and learn of Me, for I am gentle (meek) and humble (lowly) in heart, and you will find rest (relief and ease and refreshment and recreation and blessed quiet) for your souls. [Jer.6:16.] For My yoke is wholesome (useful, good – not harsh, hard, sharp, or pressing, but comfortable, gracious, and pleasant), and My burden is light and easy to be borne."* (Matthew 11:28-30, AMP)

When you come to Jesus, you are not going to feel badly about yourself because God does not feel badly about you. Again, God is not interested in beating you up. God loves you, and when you ask for forgiveness, God will not be hard, sharp and cold with you; God will only expect you to turn from the wrong and move into doing what is right.

3

Joseph's Stages of Change

The Bible says,

> "Joseph could stand it no longer. "Out, all of you!" he cried out to his attendants. He wanted to be alone with his brothers when he told them who he was. Then he broke down and wept aloud. His sobs could be heard throughout the place, and the news quickly carried to Pharaoh's palace...but don't be angry with yourselves that you did this to me, for God did it. He sent me here ahead of you to preserve your lives." (Genesis 45:1-2, 5 NLT)

Joseph's weeping was a release to let go of his bitterness and anger toward his brothers. His brothers did several cruel things to him; one was selling him into slavery. Now the emphasis should not be placed on Joseph's weeping, but his willingness to let go (forgive) his brothers of a painful and wrongful hurt.

Joseph, no doubt, knew that he could not fulfill God's will for his life being mad and upset. Joseph did not deserve what his brothers put him through. (Genesis 40:15, NLT) However, God had a plan to preserve the Israel nation in time of a seven-year famine. The nation was to be preserved through the hand of Joseph.

You need to know that every time somebody does you wrong, and every time things look like they are working against you, know that God is up to something and He will restore, heal, deliver, and set you free from all harm and worries. Just continue to trust Him (God) and stay in a spirit of love and compassion, and God will eventually turn that situation around and cause it to work in your favor.

If God can restore, in a matter of seconds to Joel, all the years that the locusts, cankerworms and other insects had destroyed (Joel 2:25), God will do the same for you. God will loose you and set you free from the thing or things that have been trying to consume and choke the life out of you. God can and will do an unheard of thing for you. That is right—God **can** and He **will do** an unheard of thing just to get you what you need.

Let us look briefly at some biblically unheard-of

things that God did for His people. **First**, look at Numbers 16:1-34, which I recommend you, read in the *Amplified Version* of the Bible to get the full grasp of what is being conveyed. In this chapter, Moses said that God was going to do a new thing to his enemies; the earth would literally open up and swallow all them who were against what Moses was doing for the Lord.

In this particular chapter, the Bible says that the ground opened…swallowing up all offenders and then, the ground returned to its original state. How can that happen? Easily, God can do it, and He will do whatever it takes to heal, deliver and protect you.

Second, in Exodus, the ninth chapter, God sent a plague of hail and fire mixed together upon the Pharaoh and the Egyptian people because they refused to let the children of Israel go from slavery. *"So there was hail, and fire, mingled with hail, very grievous, such as there was none like it in all the land of Egypt since it became a nation." (Exodus 9:24)* Now, if you ask meteorologists about fire and water mixing together, they will tell you that that is scientifically impossible. However, God can do it.

God can take a black cow; feed it green grass, and the black cow will produce white milk. God can do it; God **can** and **will** rescue your life. God is willing to do whatever it will take to show Himself strong on your behalf. (II Chronicles 16:9a)

Notice this scripture: *"He shall call upon me, and I will answer him: I will be with him in trouble; I will deliver him, and honour him. With long life will I satisfy him and shew him my salvation." (Psalms 91:15-16)*

Third, in II Kings, the sixth chapter, there we will experience another unnatural occurrence.

> *"But as one was felling his beam, the axe head fell into the water; and he cried, Alas my master, for it was borrowed! The man of God asked," Where did it fall? When shown the place, Elisha cut off a stick and threw it in the water, and the iron floated. He said, pick it up. And he put his hand and took it. (II Kings 6:5-7, AMP)*

How can an axe head swim on top of water? If you look at the physical components of what the axe head consists of, there is no way scientifically possible that an axe head is going to float on water. Nevertheless, God can do it; God can and He will restore whatever you have lost, and your situation cannot get so bad to where God cannot put things back together. God has a way of getting you what you need; trust Him and He shall bring to pass the thing that you desire.

In Genesis 45:1-2, God could not bless Joseph until he let go of his hurt. Are you holding on to anything?

If so, **the thing that you refuse to release could be the thing that keeps you from breaking free and overcoming.** Therefore, you must set your will to forgive by letting it go, no matter what.

Forgiveness is extremely important, because if you do not forgive and release people of the wrong that they have done to you, you will never enter into the best that God has for you. Notice this scripture: *"But when you are praying, first forgive anyone you hold a grudge against, so that your Father in Heaven will forgive your sins, too." (Mark 11:25 NLT)*

Hurting people has a tendency to do three things: 1) hurt themselves, 2) hurt others, and 3) make bad decisions. The reason that hurting people do these things is because they are hurting inwardly and therefore, they are only concerned with protecting themselves from being injured again emotionally. You should never make decisions when you are angry, hurting or under a lot of duress, because your thinking is not clear and the decisions you make today can affect you for a lifetime.

Pastor Gregory Dickow in his book, *How to Never be Hurt Again*, says:

> *You can get to a point where, no matter what somebody does to you, it never hurts you. You can get to the point where you can say, "I'll never be hurt another day in my life." Doesn't*

that sound liberating? We can literally be emotionally invincible. That's what God means when He says that nothing shall, by any means, hurt us. We can become invincible people. We can become people who are impenetrable. We can become people who cannot be defeated, because real destruction in our lives is not going to come from the outside. It's going to come from within; as is our success." (p.14)

In looking back at the life of Joseph, his brothers put him into a pit and then sold him into slavery at the age of 17. I am sure most people would have looked at that situation and just wrote off Joseph. (Genesis 45:26-28)

Again, God had a plan and He would work through Joseph's attitude to be a blessing to a nation of people. Many times those who enter into greatness go through extreme difficulties.

One of the major factors to overcome bad habits is that you focus on God, and not the problem. If you talk about the problem more than you talk to God, this could be considered idolatry because you are putting the problem or hurt above God. You must release the problem or hurt, and be consumed with God's word.

Through it all, Joseph stayed focused on what God

had promised him; he never wavered from it. Joseph spent 13 years in prison, but God brought him from a pit to a palace. Joseph was elevated because he was willing to forgive those who hurt him, and had a right attitude when people did him wrong.

You should deal with all people the way you would want to be treated. (Matthew 7:12) Joseph's brothers had no idea that they would see their brother again after selling him into slavery, but God did. Joseph went from a pit, to slavery, to prison to the inner prison (maximum prison) to becoming the governor of the whole land of Egypt. There was only one man in all the land of Egypt who had more power than Joseph and that was the Pharaoh, King of Egypt.

So when Joseph's brothers came to Egypt for food, they were shocked to see Joseph still alive and in a most prestigious position. Joseph could have had them all killed but God had a plan. Some of you may be going through something right now. You may be experiencing something that is no fault of your own. You might have been set up, lied to and abused, but God can reverse the curse; God can take a wrong and make it right. God can do it.

Lessons to be Learned

1) **You must let things go** (forgive) **quickly.** If you do not let them go quickly, than you will prevent God from doing what He wants to do in your life. *"And Joseph called the name of the firstborn Manasseh: For God, said he, hath made me forget all my toil, and all my father's house. And the name of the second called he Ephraim: For God hath caused me to be fruitful in the land of my affliction." (Genesis 41:51-52)*

   Before Joseph could experience the fruitfulness (Ephraim) of God's blessings he had to forget (Manasseh) those who had wronged him. Release it and let it go.

2) **What you give to people is what you are going to get back.** *"Give, and it shall be given unto you; good measure, pressed down, and shaken together, and running over, shall men give into your bosom." (Luke 6:38)* This scripture refers to more than just money; it refers to treating people with a right attitude. Many people are going through trouble and are experiencing an overflow of it because they refuse to treat people right.

3) **Look out for yourself.** *"But think on me when it shall be well with thee, and shew kindness, I pray*

thee, unto me and make mention of me unto Pharaoh, and bring me out of this house." (Genesis 40:14) It was what Joseph said that the butler remembered, which was the word *me.* This was not selfishness; in the process of helping others, make sure you do not cripple yourself. **Set limits and boundaries with people** so that you can get proper sleep and rest to fulfill the complete will of God for your life and not get burned out.

Many people experience setbacks because they fear telling the truth. They do things they do not want to do for fear of being fired from a job, talked about, misunderstood or looked down upon. The Bible indicates that Jesus was not concerned with what others thought about Him (Philippians 2:7); He was only concerned with the will of God for His life. Everything fell into place under God's will!

4) **Don't allow where you are presently to determine where you will be permanently.** *"I am Joseph your brother, whom ye sold into Egypt." (Genesis 45:4)* Joseph could have become stuck right there in the midst of his past hurts, but he refused to allow his past traumas to set him back. Joseph stayed focused and kept his eyes on what God was doing in his life, which brought him from the pit to the palace.

Again, one of the main things that made Joseph so great is that he never became bitter. He just used everything he went through to make him better. **Do not get bitter; get better.** Joseph, very easily, could have become angry with God. Also, Joseph could have become angry with his father for showing him so much favoritism over his brothers. Joseph's father's favoritism for Joseph enabled Joseph's brothers to be jealous, and provoked them to do the evil that they did.

Joseph could have become bitter at Potiphar's wife, who lied on him, and Joseph could have become bitter at Potiphar sentencing Joseph to be imprisoned, but Joseph did not become bitter at people that did him wrong. He shook it off, stepped on it and stepped up. That's what you and I have to do... we have to shake off negative thoughts, past hurts, evil desires, and wrong behaviors, and use negativity and opposition as an opportunity for advancement.

There is a story about a man who had a donkey; the man's donkey was not doing what he asked it to do. Rather than shooting the donkey, the man decided to put the donkey in a deep pit where people throw their trash, thinking that the donkey would just suffocate and die. When people began to throw their trash in the pit, the donkey shook off the trash and stepped on it. This method of the donkey continued many days. Every time someone threw his/her trash in the pit, the donkey would shake it off and step on it.

Finally, with enough shaking it off and stepping on it, the donkey was able to become so high to the point that he was able to walk right out of the mess. The point is this: you can walk out, get out and stay out of whatever keeps you down. Keep the right attitude. Don't get mad, bitter, or angry.

Notice this scripture:

> *"Therefore they did set over them taskmasters to afflict them with their burdens. And they built for Pharaoh treasure cities, Pithom and Raamses. But the more they afflicted them, the more they multiplied and grew. And they were grieved because of the children of Israel." (Exodus 1:11-12)*

The children of Israel became stronger and stronger through the hardship placed on them by the Egyptians. The children of Israel multiplied and grew under the pressure of trouble. *"A righteous man may have many troubles, but the LORD delivers him from them all." (Psalm 34:19, NIV)* In life, you will experience hard times, but that doesn't mean that you pack up and leave or quit, ignoring what God told you to do. You stay in there and believe that your situation will get better. Watch what God can do to make your situation make you better.

4

Things Most People Ignore about Letting Go

First, most people ignore the fact that, saying *I am sorry* **to a person is not enough.** You will have to stop making excuses for what you do and learn to do the right thing. When a person says that they are sorry about something, this is very good. However, saying I am sorry is not the end, but only the beginning to the process of change. Eventually, the person who apologized, must move from saying, *I am sorry,* to work on not saying and doing things that makes him/her sorry.

> *But when he saw many of the Pharisees and Sadducees come to his baptism, he said unto them, O generation of vipers, who hath warned you to flee from the wrath to come?*

Bring forth therefore fruits meet for repentance. (Matthew 3:7-8)

The word **repentance** means, in this particular verse of scriptures, a *reversal in decision* or *to change the way of thinking.* When a person truly repents, there is a change or a turn from old behavior to positive, new behavior. John the Baptist was interested in the religious leaders demonstrating manifested results (proof) that they had turned from sinning and turned to living holy and righteous for God. Therefore, John was looking for the true mark of repentance.

Some people can become addicted to making excuses; they say that they are sorry, but never demonstrate any signs to validate that they are sorry or that they have changed.

Dr. Bridget E. Hilliard, in her book, *The Will to Win,* says:

> *The major step that must be taken is the mental step of eliminating all excuses from remaining in your present, unfulfilled state. Excuses are the crutches for the uncommitted, and just beyond your excuse is the effort you need to win. Excuses are the smoke screens of the self-deceived! Unfortunately, only you feel your fabricated reason for remaining in your state is justifiable; others who know*

you know that your flimsy reason is just an excuse." (P. 9)

If a person is constantly offending another person, then the person who constantly offends needs to get help. If a person is verbally or physically abusive to someone, the abused person is not interested in you saying *I am sorry*; this person is only interested in you no longer being the abuser. Therefore, saying *I am sorry* is not enough.

Again, while it is perfectly all right to apologize, the offender must desire not to offend. Remember this; people will always remember you more for what you **do**. You can say all the right things, but end up doing all the wrong things. (Matthew 7:15–20, NLT)

5

Laws that Govern Letting Things Go

When I mention the word *law* I am referring to the law as an established set principle. A **law** is *an established principle that will work the same way every time for anyone who chooses to become involved.* Take for instance, the law of gravity. If you go up on a roof and jump off, you will come down. That's a law meaning that it is an established principle. If you choose to get involved in the established principle, it is going to work the same way no matter who you are.

Let's take a person who likes to eat all the time; if that person does not get control or gain some type of restraint over his/her eating habits, this person will continue to get bigger. The more you consume, the bigger you will become, because the law of sowing and reaping indicates that what you do is what you are going to get. Eat a lot and you get big; eat less and you get smaller.

I like what Dr. Fredrick K.C. Price, said in his book, *Faith, Foolishness or Presumption:*

> *"A lot of people have the silly ideal that they can overeat and not get fat. My wife and I were having dinner with some people one time. We could look at one girl, and tell that she was overweight. And when she prayed over the food, she cast out the calories... Praying over your food, saying, "In the name of Jesus, I cast these calories out. Come out in Jesus' Name," is pure foolishness. You need to bring your body under subjection. It's not Faith to think you can pray and eat whatever you want." (P.97, 99)*

This is why it is so important to understand the laws that govern letting things go. The law of sowing and reaping in the Bible says,

> *"Don't be misled. Remember that you can't ignore God and get away with it. You will always reap what you sow! Those who live only to satisfy their own sinful desires will harvest the consequences of decay and death. But those who live to please the Spirit will*

harvest everlasting life from the Spirit."
(Galatians 6:7-8, NLT)

I believe most people fail to realize that sowing and reaping goes beyond just giving of finances; sowing and reaping covers how you treat yourself and others. If you do well, then good will come; if you treat your body and mind in a negative manner, then you will destroy your body and corrupt your mind.

My point is whatever you do, it is going to come back at ya; if you smoke cigarettes or abuse drugs and don't quit, you will get cancer and eventually die; if you are an overeater, the law (established principle) says that you will become overweight. The only way to overcome negative activities in your life is to become involved in the law of life that is in Christ Jesus. (Romans 8:2)

The **first** thing to understand about the laws that govern letting things go is that **things just do not happen**. That is true...things just do not happen; if you are going to let things go you will have to get a plan and work the plan.

Here is a scripture example of what I mean:

"So he went and did according unto the word of the Lord: for he went and dwelt by the brook Cherith that is before Jordan. And the ravens brought him bread and flesh in the morning, and bread and flesh

in the evening; and he drank of the brook."
(I Kings 17:5-6)

The key thing to note is that Elijah did exactly what the Lord said and he prospered. Elijah had to go to the brook; God did not go for him. Again, this is generally a major oversight by many Christians, thinking that things just happen or that God is just going to bless them.

That kind of thinking is far from the truth. You will be responsible for the outcome of the decision that you make, whether good or bad, right or wrong. Ultimately, you will be responsible and God will get involved when you make the decision to do your part.

Scripture says, *"Then Isaac sowed in that land, and received in the same year an hundredfold: and the LORD blessed him." (Genesis 26:12)* Isaac was responsible for his harvest by sowing. When he sowed, it allowed God to get involved by putting his Hand on his seed that was sown, which enabled Isaac to receive a hundred times what he gave.

You have to give God something to work with *"...But be ye doers of the word, and not hearers only, deceiving your own selves." (James 1:22)* The old saying is *"you can lead a horse to water, but you can't make him drink."* In other words, the horse has to decide for itself whether or not to drink the water. God gave Elijah the strength to go to the brook; however, Elijah had to settle in his mind that he was going to put forth the effort and go.

If the Prophet Elijah had not gone to the brook, he would have died of starvation...just like everyone else. However, Elijah put forth the effort to get there and God gave him the strength to get there. Everything that Elijah needed was right there at the brook because he was right where he was appointed to be. This same thing will happen in your life when you put forth the effort to get to where you are supposed to be. God will give you everything that you need.

⑥

Forgiving the Klu Klux Klan

I remember one racist event that occurred in my home-town Shelby, North Carolina. I was out of Bible College for the summer and had just returned home from missionary work in India. I was at the Cleveland County Library, minding my own business when an older woman who I would see occasionally in the library came up to me. She was shaking considerably and said," *Young man, have you heard, have you heard, the Klu Klux Klan is up town, the Klu Klux Klan is up town.*" Then the woman just took off.

As I was reading my book, I began to think about the Klu Klux Klan being up town, and how I had never visibly seen a Klu Klux Klan rally. So, I closed my book and headed up town to observe what was going on.

When I arrived up town with my car windows rolled down, I noticed that the grand dragon or the captain was saying things like, the nigger this and the nigger that. He was speaking through a microphone publicly in the town square in front of many police officers and citizens of Shelby. He was saying that niggers are to be hated, and Jews were not people, and the sad thing was no one was doing anything about it.

This event was very demoralizing to me as a young adult. I was torn. I became bitter at whites, especially officers, because here were law officials permitting hate advocators to speak derogatorily and racially against other races of people because of color and national-ity, and the law officers were allowing it to happen. I thought to myself, how in the world this could be justifiable.

It is also important to note that up until this time I had no education on black history. In my days of elementary and high school, I never heard any of my teachers talk about Afro-American history. Although I am fully aware that they have black history classes in high school now, at that time, my high school had no black history classes.

I remember one of my high school history teachers saying that, although Abraham Lincoln initiated the Emancipation Proclamation, he was not for the free-ing of black slaves. I find it to be very interesting how some recent reports, political leaders, teachers and even preachers are extremely quick to educate people on the history of World War I and II, Pearl Harbor, Adolf Hitler, Saddam Hussein, and other massive killings.

Very seldom, if at all, do these same people talk about all the blacks who were killed right here in America from slavery. I believe one of the reasons is because people do not like to deal with themselves; people are more prone to look at others' issues than to face one's own.

In the book, *The Words of Martin Luther King, Jr.,* says,

> *"It is pretty difficult to like some people. Like is sentimental and it is pretty difficult to like someone bombing your home; it is pretty difficult to like somebody threatening your children; it is difficult to like congressmen who spend all of their time trying to defeat civil rights. But Jesus says love them, and love is greater than like." (P.23)*

I knew that God was not a racist; my mother did not raise my family to be racist; she taught us to love all people regardless of color or nationality. It was at this point that I really began to grow up spiritually and come to the realization that the world needed Jesus. Scripture says, *"God so loved the world, that he gave his only begotten Son, that whosoever believeth in him should not perish, but have everlasting life." (John 3:16)*

God loves every human being; God's love is demonstrated by how we deal with other people.

Love never hates, discriminates, or even isolates because of a person's skin color. Therefore, I just could not understand why these white men would hide behind white sheets and tell the American citizens of Shelby, North Carolina that they were better than other people.

What they said sparked a righteous indignation in me toward hatred and racism. It really did not matter to me who the Klu Klux Klan were talking about, to preach hatred in public was wrong. Better yet, to teach and preach hatred period is wrong and should be considered a crime regardless of who you are. It does not matter if you are white, black or in between, if you are teaching or preaching hatred, it is wrong.

In his book, *Race, Religion and Racism*, Dr. Fredrick, K.C. Price, says,

> *"We get upset, righteously indignant – and correctly so – when we think about Adolf Hitler and the annihilation of six million Jews during World War II. But who gets righteously indignant and upset about the fifty million black Africans who were abducted or killed by the forefathers of this nation?" (P.164)*

When I arrived up town, I heard the Klu Klux Klan preaching hate and no one doing anything about it. Again, I had a righteous indignation. When my feet hit the ground after getting out of my car, immediately I began to shout aloud, *"Jesus Christ is Lord, Jesus Christ is Lord, Jesus Christ is Lord!"* I walked up and down about a block saying Jesus Christ is Lord. Everyone became quiet, including the Klu Klux Klan. You could hear a pin drop on the town square.

Immediately, three officers came running over to me. Yelling and saying as they approached me, "Hey! Hey! Hey! You cannot do that, you cannot do that, you are going to start a riot," of course that was definitely not my intention to start a riot. One of the officers was a white female and the others were white males. They told me that if I did not stop saying that, they were going to put me in jail.

I walked about another ten feet or so, communicating nothing but Jesus Christ is Lord, Jesus Christ is Lord. It was as though I could not stop. My adrenaline was flowing. I felt that I was experiencing a glimpse of what the prophet Ezekiel experienced when saying that the spirit of the Lord came on him and took him away. (Ezekiel 8:3, 37:1) I believe that this taking away was literally in the spirit to where they had no control over what was being done unto them, until the spirit had completed the mission through them.

As I was walking back to my car, a very elderly woman came up to me and said, *"Young man, young man, I want you to know that what you did was of God."* This elderly woman continued to say, *"When you were speaking a holy hush came over the whole place and the only thing you could hear was Jesus Christ is Lord."*

I indicated to this elderly woman that I was walking to my car and I would like to talk with her more, but when I returned from my car this woman was gone. She had not stood that far away from me. I estimated she had stood maybe 20 or 25 yards away. Therefore, I proceeded to walk down the block, but the elderly woman was nowhere around.

There was a small alley. I thought maybe this elderly woman could have possibly walked down the alley, but as I walked down the alley, no one was there. I knew that this elderly woman could not have run all the way down the alley without me seeing her. Therefore, I considered this elderly woman to be an angel of the Lord who was protecting me from any danger that could have occurred.

That night at home, I began to reflect upon my day. I asked the Lord why He used me to do something like that. This is what God revealed to me about the situation: First, everyone who was at the town square that day, who did not accept Jesus as Lord and personal Savior, they would be without excuse when they stand before God on Judgment Day, including the Klu Klux Klan.

The Lord continued to say, all who heard that Jesus Christ is Lord that day, will not be able to say that they did not hear and know the truth on judgment day. God continued to say to me to set that particular day aside as a memorial before heaven, the preaching of an unlearned, young black man, from Shelby, North Carolina making a mark in history that would be remembered before all eternity.

God continued to reveal to me that what the Klu Klux Klan had thought was going to be a motivational hate rally, God set it up to be a <u>day of remembrance</u>, which all who heard would be without excuse. In addition, it was clearly obvious to me that some people heard, because about no more than five minutes after I had spoken, the Klu Klux Klan began tearing down their set and everyone started to leave.

In Luke 16:19-31, the Bible talks about a beggar who went to Heaven and a rich man who went to Hell. The rich man went to Hell, and in Hell this rich man was able to remember all the times he had an opportunity to get it right with God. Although, this rich man was in Hell, he remembered those times. Therefore, he could not use the excuse that he did not know.

Interestingly, when this rich man saw that he could not get out of Hell, he immediately remembered that he had five brothers alive at home who were living just as he had been living. The rich man begged for special treatments, signs and enlightenments to come to his brothers, in hope that these events will cause them to change, to prevent them from coming to the same place of torment.

The answer to the rich man's request was, *"They have Moses and the prophets: let them hear them."* Moses signified the pastor and the prophet symbolizes the spokesperson for God. The rich man learned that if your brothers do not listen and take heed to the pastors of the local church or the evangelist, preacher or teacher of the Gospel of Jesus Christ, then surely, they would not be convinced nor have cause to hear anyone else—even if God raised a prophet from the dead to speak to them.

It is important to understand that you cannot let other people's hatred become your hatred. Throughout my young adulthood, I allowed this to happen to me. The more I would try to get away from white people the more God would put me in their setting.

I attended a predominately white church in Shelby, North Carolina. I attended a predominately white bible college in Charlotte, North Carolina. I attended a predominately white seminary in Cleveland, Tennessee, and I attended one year of CPE (clinical pastoral education) in a predominately white setting. So the question in all of that is this, what was God trying to teach me? God was teaching me that I had to let go of my past hurt. Just because some white people did me wrong growing up does not mean that all white people are evil.

God taught me that no one owes me anything. When you forgive a person you forgive them of all things. I also learned that it is sin to hold someone responsible for something that the person had no control over. It is also sin to hold a white person responsible for slavery when he/she was not even born during the period of slavery or had any association with that time period.

I learned that where I was in life was actually where I chose to be. I could not blame the white man, slavery, and a lack of education or any unjust act for where I was in life. God began to teach me that He set me around white people because I had the ability to let things go, forgive, love, heal, restore and build a bridge to where whites and blacks could work together to achieve more, than to work against each other and receive less.

As I continued to work in a multicultural setting, I learned that not all white people were bad and that white people learned from me that not all blacks are evil. I learned to understand the true meaning of the word team. The word team means *together everyone achieves much*.

Joyce Meyer in her book, *Reduce me to Love,* says, *"When we forgive an injustice, we are actually doing ourselves a favor; we are giving ourselves a gift of freedom." (P.122)* God expects us to love everybody regardless of what they do to us. In order to love others you must first love God. He will enable you to love yourself, so that you can love others. If you do not love yourself, you cannot love others. You cannot give away something that you do not have.

One of the things about hate is that when you hold on to it you are troubling yourself. The only way to have true peace in your life is to have the love of God in your heart. In addition, you should not expect any scriptures whatsoever to work for you when you are not walking in love. Every promise of God hangs on love, and without love you can do nothing for God. Love is the first and greatest commandment.

Notice this scripture:

> *Jesus said unto him, Thou shalt love the Lord thy God with all thy heart, and with all thy soul, and with all thy mind. This is the first and great commandment. And the second is like unto it, Thou shalt love thy neighbor as thyself. On these two commandments hang all the law and the prophets. (Matthew 22:37-40)*

Dr. Creflo Dollar, in his book, *The Color of Love,* says,

> "As Christian people, when Jesus said, **Love your enemies,** He meant all of them – our black enemies and our white enemies, too. When he said, **Do good to them that hate you,** He didn't say you were to do good to everybody – except for that white man or that black man. You are walking in strong deception if you think you can call yourself a Christian, whether white or black, and still feel hatred toward that brother or sister whom you see every day." (P. 8)

The last thing that God shared with me about preaching to the KKK is that I was preaching from a wounded spirit. God indicated to me that my message was one that was crying out for help. It hurt me when I was hearing those hate words and it moved me to action in a non-judgmental response by saying that Jesus Christ is Lord.

God indicated to me that He really appreciated my zeal; however, my zeal would have to move to a place to where I could sit down with people of various races and nationalities to work out racial differences. We were to explore past history, and to work through misconceptions about different races so that we could work together to reach the world for Jesus Christ.

One of the tools that the devil uses against society today is to keep the different races of people separated. When people choose not to explore their differences, we limit ourselves. There is a lot that whites can learn from blacks and blacks can learn from whites, but we must put our racial prejudices down and embrace multicultural togetherness.

We need men and women of God who are willing to look beyond color and reach out to the needy, no matter who they are. If there is a need, as Christians we are to meet the need. This is what we need in the body of Christ today.

It does not matter what peoples past hang-ups, setbacks, or addictions are, God is calling every born-again Christian to love, and to reach out to a dying and lost world for Jesus Christ. To take it a step further, it does not matter what peoples present hang-ups, setbacks or addictions are, God has still called every born-again Christian to love the hell (Gehenna) out of people.

7

Demonic Decoys

I remember going to work on a particular day, and this day was a very challenging day; things were not working as well as they should. Therefore, I began to pray and meditate on the word of God to myself as I worked. That evening I received a phone call from a co-worker who was very upset. His words were very unpleasant; it was obvious to me that this person was having some issues.

I felt disrespected, and began to share some of my concerns with this person. That was a big mistake! Instead of the situation getting better, it became worse. Later that evening, I called this person and tried to resolve what was wrong.

I experienced the same thing, nothing different than when we had spoken the first time. This person was even more disrespectful and refused to help resolve what was wrong. After I finished talking with the person, I just continued to pray, listening to inspirational Christian music.

The next day at home, I woke up still praying in the Holy Spirit, listening to inspirational Christian music and reading the word of God. I prepared for the home-going that would take place at church later that afternoon.

I arrived at the church an hour before the event, praying in the Holy Spirit and full of the word of God. We gathered together all of the volunteers to pray for the service. After, we, the volunteers, had prayed for the service, we continued setting up for the home-going service. As we were arranging things for the service, we continued to pray softly to ourselves in the Holy Spirit.

As a result of our praying in the Spirit, people began to come through the door, the Spirit of God began to move, people were being healed, comforted, strengthened and encouraged by the volunteers. We received so many compliments that day on how good a job we were doing.

After the eulogy, the minister gave an altar call or an invitation for those who would like to accept Jesus Christ as Lord and Savior to come forth. That day we had 115 young people come down and accept Jesus Christ as Lord and personal Savior of their lives!

God revealed to me that the confusion on the job was just a demonic decoy. A demonic decoy is evil spirits creating confusion in the spirit, mind and body of a person. A demonic decoy is designed to strictly distract; it causes you to lose focus of your spiritual assignment, with the intention of you never fulfilling the God-intended purpose for your life.

I learned that keeping some things to yourself is much better when negative thoughts occur in your mind. In most cases, if you observe certain negative things that are going on around you, God has revealed it to you so that you can pray about it, not talk about it to others.

When there is no apparent reason for things to be chaotic or discombobulated, do not get frustrated, because God is about to do something great in your life. When there appears to be intense struggle and extreme agitation in your life, go deeper in the word of God and prayer.

Jesus instructs Peter: *"...Now go out where it is deeper and let down your nets, and you will catch many fish." (Luke 5:4, NLT)* When Peter obeyed the instructions of Jesus and entered into the deep, he came up with some great results. He caught more fish than he could even imagine. As Christians, we are to walk in this same mentality. It makes no difference what is going on with you; God is going to do something great, awesome, and very significant in your life.

Things are going to happen to you that you do not like. Just stay focused and keep moving in the direction that God is leading you. Stay in a spirit of love and forgiveness, and do not be stuck in the defensive mode. Stay humble, be kind and keep heading toward what your God-given spiritual assignment is to be.

This co-worker of mine was not in a position to receive anything I had to say. This person was so self-absorbed that nothing that I said mattered to him. It is important that you recognize this type of behavior and stay away from it. The Bible says, *"Make no friend-ship with an angry man; And with a furious man thou shalt not go: Lest thou learn his way, And get snare to thy soul." (Proverbs 22:24-25)*

Walking in the love of God is one of the best ways to calm an angry spirit, although, it is up to the individual to change. Love will have a profound effect on the angry person to where he/she will sense a need to change. There is a song that says, *"Love lifted me, love lifted me, when nothing else could help love lifted me."*

When you love a person who is unloving, it is the love of God that the unloving person will see and it is the love of God that will lift the unloving person up out of anger. One of the best ways to deal with an angry man is to love him. Love can climb the highest mountain and penetrate the toughest heart. It is love that will lift you up when you are feeling down. Love will never fail. (I Corinthians 13:8)

It is important to pray and walk in the love of God because some things can catch you off guard. My co-worker's negative behavior initially felt like a bomb exploding; however, because I understood the strategies of a demonic decoy, I quickly got myself in the love of God to keep both the peace of God and the blessing of God upon my life. Now, I am here to say that it was love that lifted me.

Moreover, God showed me how we, the volunteers, played a great role in the 115 young people coming to the Lord. God revealed that because the volunteers arrived an hour early, we were able to set the atmosphere for the Holy Spirit to do great things at the home-going celebration.

Because of the volunteers praying in the Holy Spirit, we were tearing down strong holds, taking authority over the spirit of grief and depression, and creating an atmosphere for the people to be delivered, healed, set free, made whole, and to become born-again.

8

Church Makes a Difference

I remember attending a particular Church in Charlotte, North Carolina, and at the end of the message the pastor gave an altar call. The pastor asked if anyone needed to accept Jesus Christ as Lord and personal Savior to come forward, or if anyone needed to rededicate his/her life back to Jesus, join the church or if anyone just needed prayer. A Christian, who was knowledgeable in praying for people, would pray for those who came down front.

There were many people who came forth for the altar call, so the pastor asked me to help. A young, black male came down who appeared to be in his mid 30's. I asked the young man what he would like prayer for. The young man said, "You do not want to know what I am thinking about doing." I shared with the young man, "Sure, I do, and there is nothing too hard for God." (Job 42:1-2)

This young man informed me that he was getting ready to leave the church to kill a man. I did not get into the whys and wherefores with this particular young man because I was a visiting minister; I prayed and referred him to the pastor and certain administrative personnel of the church which was trained to handle this kind of situation.

To make a long story short, this young man, after a Spirit led directed prayer, accepted Jesus Christ as Lord and his personal Savior. Not only did this young man become born-again, but he was filled with the Holy Ghost with the evidence of speaking in tongues. This man left the altar with a changed mind. The yoke of homicidal ideation was broken. This young man left saved, healed, delivered and set free.

How can someone tell me that the church does not work! How can someone tell me that prayer does not work! How can someone tell me that the word of God does not work! Oh yes, they work! You might not be doing your part right. If you have not tried church, prayer or the Word, then stay silent. You don't know how church, prayer and the word of God works.

As I look back over my life experiences, God gave me the strength, knowledge and desire to overcome every-thing negative that I had to endure. God brought me out. God rescued, delivered and set me free. I learned that God would use the church to help me overcome bad habits and break chronic addictions.

God would use the praise and worship leaders to sing the right songs; God would use the assistant ministers to teach and preach messages that would reach me exactly where I was in life, and God would use greeters to smile, give hugs when appropriate and to say words of kindness. God will do the same for you if you go to church.

9

Naaman's Acceptance

A good biblical example of a person being open and willing to accept change can be located in II Kings 5:19. Naaman, a leper, was instructed by the Prophet Elisha to wash himself seven times in the river of Jordan to be healed of his leprosy. This procedure is important because if freedom, breakthroughs, healing, promotion and increase is going to take place in your life, you must be willing to listen and to carry out the instruction that has been given to you.

Now you would think after hearing the words of a prophet of God, you would go forth and do what is said— not so with Naaman. He was very egotistical. However, after being persuaded by his servant that he had nothing to lose, Naaman let go of his egoism and did as Elisha instructed.

If you are going to be restored, to be set free, and to

overcome, you have to release or let go of your ego. You must put your opinions down and do what is required for the process of healing to take place. Whatever God tells you to do, do it, because His instruction is going to work whether or not you feel like it.

Another important thing to note is **God will often work through people to give you what you need**. God has always used mankind as a vehicle to transport His goods. Therefore, you have to listen to spiritual authority, the doctors, the weight instructors, those who are trained, qualified, and placed in a position to help you get better.

If things are going to get better for you… and trust me… things **will** get better, you need to listen and carry out the instructions to make you better. Naaman settled it within himself that he was going to do what was instructed and gave it a try. As a direct result of him listening to the spiritual advisor, he was healed of his leprosy.

His change came because he did what he did not want to do. Naaman was very fortunate that he received his healing. Sometimes people let the answer to what they are going through pass them by. If you do not move in the proper time, you can miss everything that can make the situation right.

Naaman thought that because of his prestigious position and status as a General over the Syrian nation, his position qualified him to have special treatment. One of the reasons that Naaman did not want to submerse himself in the Jordan River is because it was not as clean as some other surrounding rivers.

Naaman preferred to be submersed in the clean surrounding rivers; he felt dipping in a dirty river would make him look bad because he was supposedly, "the Man." Naaman failed to realize that his healing was not in the water that he would wash in, but in the obedience of following God's instructions.

Scripture says, *"For if ye be willing and obedient, ye will eat the good of the land." (Isaiah 1:19)* You must do it God's way if you are going to see the results of the manifestation of change.

In his book, *If You Need Healing Do These Things,* Oral Roberts refers to Naaman:

> *"It takes a humble spirit for one to change like that. This is a marvelous thing. It doesn't take long for a man to change if he wants to. But he must want to. When he accepts God's correction, the Spirit of Christ enters him and he is a "new creation" – old things are passed away; behold, all things are become new (2 Corinthians 5:17). Repentance is a change of mind before it becomes a change of heart. General Naaman gave the order and*

they went to the river. With Elisha's message
ringing in his ears, go and wash, he plunged
into the muddy, yellow water of the famous
river Jordan. As he did so, there were only
a few ripples on the water revealing that the
great man was all under." (P. 45)

Often, people cannot overcome difficult situations because they become defensive, angry or resistant when they are confronted with their negative activity. Some people will go as far as trying to use reverse manipulation, attempting to make it appear that something is wrong with you, as an attempt to run away from their own issues.

Again, you cannot run from problems. You have to be open and willing to let things go for positive things to occur. Peter is a good example of a person being open and willing to do things differently in order to produce the results that he desires.

The Bible says:

"When He had stopped speaking, He said to
Simon (Peter), Put out into the deep [water],
and lower your nets for a haul, And Simon
(Peter) answered, Master, we toiled all night
[exhaustingly] and caught nothing [in our
nets]. But on the ground of Your word, I will
lower the nets [again]. And when they had

done this, they caught a great number of fish; and as their nets were [at the point of] breaking, They signed to their partners in the other boat to come and take hold with them, And they came and filled both the boats, so that they began to sink." (Luke 5:4-7, AMP)

If Peter had been rebellious to Jesus' words, Peter would have missed or never experienced the blessing that Jesus had for him. I believe that many people are missing certain breakthroughs and having great difficulties overcoming bad habits because they have a problem with confrontation. Confrontation is never to be feared—especially when it is coming from some one who is trying to be a blessing to you, and you know that this person has your best interest in mind.

Confronting your issues is important in overcoming tough things because if you dismiss the truth, you will be blind to what can set you free. In order to receive truth you will have to open yourself to receive what has been told to you.

"Wherefore lay apart all filthiness and superfluity of naughtiness, and receive with meekness the engrafted word, which is able to save your soul." (James 1:21)

It will be to your advantage to receive constructive criticism because being willing to hear the constructive criticism will save your soul. Therefore, you will have to put aside your pride and let go of your ego and become sensitive to the truth so that you are open to do what can make you better. Then, and only then, will you overcome your difficult times.

10

Jonah's Stages to Change

In the book of Jonah, God told Jonah to go unto Nineveh and preach repentance to the city. However, Jonah refused. He got on a boat and headed into the opposite direction. The reason for Jonah refusing to go to Nineveh is that **he was dealing with an unforgiving attitude**. He refused to forgive (let go) Nineveh for their brutal treatment toward other nations.

This is one of the main reasons why people cannot be healed of sickness and recover from diseases is because they have not let go of a wrong that was done to them. You cannot hold on to mistreatment. You must give it over to God or it will give you over to a life full of heartaches, misery and pain.

Nineveh, during Jonah's day, was considered a powerhouse city; it contained strong people. Nineveh used very ferocious and inhumane techniques of torture and could gain rapid information from captives very easily. Jonah, no doubt, knew this fact. He hoped this nation would not repent so that God could show no mercy or forgiveness.

Forgiveness is often one of the stages that must be addressed if people are going to change their behavior. Notice this scripture: *"But if ye do not forgive, neither will your father which is in heaven forgive your trespasses." (Mark 11:26)* People often wonder why bad things happen to them. It could be their unwillingness to forgive which is causing them to make inaccurate decisions. Jonah's unwillingness to forgive almost cost him his life.

God sent a tremendous windstorm to where the storm began to tear the boat into pieces. Through the process of elimination, the men on the boat found out that brother Jonah was the problem. In an attempt to try to make it better, it got worse.

This leads to the next major point. **You cannot make people change; they must be willing to change for themselves.** These men on the boat exhausted themselves trying to make the situation better. *"Instead, the sailors tried even harder to row the boat ashore. But the stormy sea was too violent for them, and they couldn't make it." (Jonah 1:13, NLT)*

Often, church leaders and counselors become burned out and drained in a needless effort to get people to change. It does not matter how much they plead with people...the church leaders and counselors could sing until the cows come home. If people's minds don't change, then change will not occur. In fact, many times people's situations will get worse before they get better, making the people ripe for change.

The next stage to Jonah's change is that he located himself. If you are going to change, you must **locate yourself**. Jonah understood what was going on around him and why it was happening to him. Jonah identified the contributing factor that was causing the storm. Think about this for a moment...if you are traveling out of town and need directions to your destination, you have to know where you are in order to get to your desired destination.

Dr Creflo A. dollar, in his book, *Claim Your Victory Today*, says,

> *Before you can expect to get from the problem to the answer, you must first clearly define and understand the exact nature of the problem you are facing. Is it Spiritual? Physical? Financial? Emotional? Whatever it is, the first step in conquering it is facing it head-on and identifying what it truly is. (P.19)*

When you locate yourself you are identifying the problem that is causing you to do what you do. *"My people are destroyed for lack of knowledge" (Hosea 4:6).* When people locate themselves, not only are they identifying problems but in some cases they recognize and are clearly aware of the contributing factors that are causing the problems.

What I mean by contributing factors is narrowing down what is happening to you. You will know and have a good understanding of exactly what is going on with you. You will work on you and not anyone else. Your focus point for change is all about you.

Notice this scripture:

> *"Wherefore, my beloved, as ye have always obeyed, not as in my presence only, but now much more in my absence, work out your own salvation with fear and trembling."* *(Philippians 2:12)*

In order to correctly get to where you are trying to go, you must know where you are at the present. You must know where you are in order to get to where you need to be. Jonah located himself: *"Throw me into the sea, Jonah said, and it will become calm again. For I know that this terrible storm is all my fault." (Jonah 1:12 NLT)*

I think it would be very important for me to say this before we continue; **wrong associations with people can produce hindrances and distractions toward**

your destination. One reason why people go through a considerable amount of trouble is because they have the wrong people around them. You must let go of all wrong relationships and associations.

The only way these mariners' lives could get back to normal was to throw Jonah overboard. This action indicates that there are some people and things in your life that you will need to throw overboard. Often, struggles and difficulties will not go until you get out of them. In most cases, your situation will get worse if you do not get out.

I drive a car that needed the brakes repaired. When I discovered this needed repair, I thought it was only minor. So I waited a little. When I took my car to the auto mechanic, he diagnosed the problem as major. Not only did I need new brakes, but also I needed new rotors.

If I would have dealt with the original problem immediately, the brake problem would not have been so bad. If I had dealt with it when I felt it needed to be looked at, the result would not have been that bad. In life, you cannot allow things to just go on and on. If you do not fix the problem, it will get so bad until the problem gets worse. What do you need to fix in your life? I would strongly suggest you fixing it immediately.

"While he yet spake, there came from the ruler of the synagogue's house which said, Thy daughter is dead: why troublest thou the Master any further? As soon as Jesus heard the word that was spoken, he saith unto the ruler of the synagogue, Be not afraid, only believe." (Mark 5: 35-36)

Why did Jesus immediately say to the ruler, only believe? Jesus knew that if the ruler had allowed negative talk of doubt and unbelief to go unchecked, the ruler would not have had the faith to see his daughter raised from the dead. Therefore, Jesus dealt with the unbelief quickly; straightened out the ruler's mindset immediately so that he could experience the power of God resurrecting the dead.

As we continue to study Jonah, he is a primary case of a person being arrogant about what he knew until **his stubbornness caused him not to change.** The fact that he was able to locate himself was good, which means that he was aware of his situation and had accepted the responsibility for what was occurring in his life and was not willing to shift the blame towards someone else. However, the fact that he was not willing to change was not so good. This is why: Not only did his flamboyant arrogance almost cost him his life, but it also almost cost innocent lives around him.

Many times, people just need to stop fooling around and do what they need to do, so that they do not have to put up with negative stuff for so long. A good example of this would be in regards to the men who were on the boat with Jonah. The Bible says,

> *"And he said unto them, Take me up, and cast me forth into the sea; so shall the sea be calm unto you: for I know that for my sake this great tempest is upon you. Nevertheless the men rowed hard to bring it to land, but they could not; for the sea wrought, and was tempestuous against them" (Jonah 1:12 -13)*

I believe that God was setting forth, as an example from brother Jonah and the mariners, that it makes no difference how hard you try to do something if it is not God's will. It makes no difference how hard you try—it just isn't going to work.

Notice this scripture, *EXCEPT THE LORD build the house, they labour in vain that build it: except the LORD keep the city, the watchman waketh but in vain. (Psalms 127:1)*

As hard as these men tried to bring the boat to land during the sea storm, they could not. It became a fruitless effort until they finally realized that the only way their situation was going to get better was for them to do what they did not want to do, which was to throw Jonah overboard. They finally stop rowing, threw Jonah overboard and immediately the problem stopped; the wind ceased, and their victory came.

So the question is, why did these men continue to row so hard when they did not have to? The bottom line is this: They were stubborn. These men were what you would call good spirited; they were some good ol' boys— they wanted the best for Jonah—which was good.

The problem is that they were attempting a task that they knew they could not do, which made it bad. They needed to let it go. They needed to let go of the thought that they was going to make it to land with Jonah on the boat. These men on the boat had good intentions toward Jonah but just made bad decisions.

They had the answer and knew what was causing the problem, yet they still tried to do something that they were incapable of doing. This is called stubbornness. There comes a time when you have to be honest with yourself and others by letting them know that what you are trying to accomplish is just not working.

The Bible says,

> *"Then Jesus used this illustration: A man planted a fig tree in his garden and came again to see if there was any fruit on it, but he was always disappointed. Finally, he said to his gardener, 'I've waited three years, and*

there hasn't been a single fig! Cut it down.
It's taking up space we can use for something
else.' The gardener answered, 'Give it one
more chance. Leave it another year, and I'll
give it special attention and plenty of fertil-
izer. If we get figs next year, fine. If not, you
can cut it down.' " (Luke 13:6-9, NLT)

If things are not working for you, maybe you should not be doing what you are doing or maybe you need to do something different. (Luke 13:6-9, NLT) There comes a time when you have to submit what you are going through to God. Submitting to God is precisely what these men on the boat eventually did. They finally threw Jonah overboard. Then peace and calm arrived. We need to get with God's programs **immediately** to avoid unnecessary struggles.

I often watch the game of baseball and observe how the manger will take the pitcher out of the game. If the pitcher continues to make mistakes, especially if it is a tight game and they need the win, the manger will get that player out immediately.

On the contrary, in the Body of Christ, we do things and know that the things we are doing are not working, yet, we still stick to what we are doing. We have to stop that. We must have the mentality of the baseball manger; if it's not working then we have to step up to the plate and switch it up or do something different.

After Jonah was thrown overboard at his request, the sea became calm and then a great fish swallowed up Jonah. (Jonah 1:17) Now Jonah goes through hell, hitting the bottom in order to become ripe for change. **Hitting the bottom** is when a person experiences a major crisis knocking him/her off balance, enabling the individual to look at things differently, taking a deep honest inventory of himself/herself, which ultimately causes this person to change.

This idea should serve as a good point because we should not be too quick to bail people out. These folks on the boat lost almost everything trying to save Jonah, and the truth of the matter is, that nothing could have saved Jonah but himself. Jonah needed to get right with God, meaning that Jonah would have had to repent, to change and let go, and then do exactly what God was asking him to do.

For things to get better for you, you must let go of past hurts and disappointments. Come unto me is the word of Jesus and He will give the troubled rest. (Matthew 11:28) However, this is something that **you** have to do. *Come to Jesus.* He is the way to get you out of your trouble. (John 14:6)

If Jonah refused to obey God, nothing was going to help him except for Jonah hitting bottom. This fact is important because I have seen people unwilling to repent of sins while church leaders pray for change. Nothing happens...because the person refuses to do what he/she knows is right.

It is important to have a non-anxious presence with people. A **non-anxious presence** means *that you will sit actively patient with people but you will not move too quickly to bail people out*; you will demonstrate a genuine interest in their concern. However, you must be aware that you are not responsible to fix people's problems—only God can do that. You are responsible to relay the truth so that people can know what to do in order to fix the problem.

I think it is interesting that these mariners or the men on the ship, after they threw Brother Jonah overboard, released Jonah to God. They said a prayer for Jonah; however, they kept on going to their destination. This is not insensitivity; you should pray for people, but do not let people take you down in their mess. Release them to God. **God can do more for a person in five minutes than what you can do in a lifetime**.

Again, now Jonah goes through hell, hitting the bottom, in order to become ripe for change. Notice what he said in *Jonah 2:2 "And said, I cried by reason of mine affliction unto the LORD, and he heard me; Out of the belly of hell cried I, and thou heardest my voice;"* this was a fact that Jonah was at his lowest... he was scared and frightened to death.

This was a good stage in Jonah's life. Again, this idea is not insensitivity. Jonah refused to repent and let the past mistreatment of Nineveh go, which resulted in Jonah hitting the bottom to become vulnerable. This point of his life was the best chance for change and for him to reflect upon what God had asked him to do. In the midst of his pain, there was hope and promise for Jonah to fulfill the will of God for his life.

Finally, the **acknowledgement of wrong and the confession to make it right** was all a part of the method that Jonah used to recover from his life- threatening situation. Confession has always been known as a person's way of releasing emotional baggage.

If a tea kettle remains over the fire with the lid and cap on, there is no doubt that you will have a mess on your hands because it will explode. This action is what many people do when they have a lot of stress and pressure on them. If they do not get the mess out, they will explode. They will injure themselves and their loved ones. However, when the cap is taken off, the steam releases the pressure and the pressure in the tea kettle decreases.

In order to overcome tough times you must let go of people's wrong doings to you and find someone who you can talk with who can help you emotionally drain the pressures of life. You must find a means of release.

Jonah went to God in his time of crisis. God heard

and delivered him. (Jonah 2:2, 10) God will do the same thing for you and me today, if we will only come to God and allow Him to deliver us from all our fears.

Things to Consider about Jonah

First, God will speak to you when you are in a right relationship with Him, but when you refuse to obey Him; God will become silent to you and will not speak again until you obey Him. After God spoke to Jonah the first time to go unto Nineveh, Jonah willfully refused. God never spoke to him again, until Jonah made up his mind that he was going to do what he knew God wanted him to do.

Notice this scripture:

> *Then the word of the Lord came to Jonah the second time: "Get up! Go to the great city of Nineveh and preach the message that I will tell you." So Jonah got up and went to Nineveh according to the LORD'S command. (Jonah 3:1-3, HCSB)*

The second time God spoke to Jonah, God said the same thing that He had told Jonah the first time...get up and go to Nineveh. Jonah went through all types of problems, literally going through Hell, because he did not do what the word of the Lord instructed him to do the first time.

When Jonah made a decision to let things go and to do what God said the first time, he was able to hear the voice of God very clearly. Some people cannot hear God at all, nor can they overcome strongholds in their lives because they are not doing what God has instructed them to do. Which is to let it go.

If Jonah had not gone to Nineveh the second time, God would not have spoken to Jonah about doing anything else in the ministry because he had not done the first thing that was required by God.

The Bible says,

> *Nevertheless I have this against you, that you have left your first love. Remember therefore from where you have fallen; repent and do the first works, or else I will come to you quickly and remove your lampstand from its place – unless you repent. (Revelations 2:4-5, NKJV)*

In this passage of scripture, Jesus was indicating to the Church of Ephesus that He really appreciated their hard labor and patience to the gospel. However, He was very concerned for them because they had fallen away in their commitment to Him. God gave them an admonishment to return to their first work...to love God with all your heart. (Matthew 22:37-38)

The church at Ephesus was very busy warring off pretenders and false doctrines that were trying to infiltrate the Church by the Nicolaitans; they were working hard doing the things of God but they were not spending quality time with God, mainly because their focus had shifted from God to the Nicolaitans. Therefore, Jesus encouraged Ephesus not to forget that their great ministry service is to first minister unto the Lord.

The Interpreter's Dictionary of the Bible says,

> *Nothing is confidently known about the Nicolaitans beyond John's references to them. Their works are hated, but not described, in the letter to Ephesus. In Pergamum their teaching is held in like manner to those who held the teaching of BALAAM (Num. 25:1-2; 31:16; II Peter. 2:15; Jude 11). In early OT days Balaam had taught Balak, the Moabite king, to cause the Israelites to fall into fornication and idolatry. These same sins were taught and practiced by the Nicolaitans. (P. 547-548)*

Jesus said for the Ephesians to not get so consumed with what the Nicolaitans were doing and lose sight of what God was doing. One of the ways to combat against the spirit of error is just preach and teach the truth.

You do not have to try to defend the gospel of Jesus Christ—just live and proclaim it and everything else will be exposed to the truth.

One reason why people cannot advance to the next level in life is because of them struggling to let things go; they have not done the first thing that God has asked them to do. God is not like the restaurant Burger King...you cannot have it your way, especially, when God is requiring you to do something specifically His way.

The awesome thing about God's way is that His way is **always** the best way. His way might take you a little longer to get to where you want to be, but you can rest assured, that you **will** get there. When you arrive where God wants you, no one can ever tell you that he/she got you there.

> *But Abram said to king of Salem, I have raised my hand to the LORD, God Most High, the Possessor of heaven and earth, that I will take nothing, from a thread to a sandal strap, and that I will not take anything that is yours, lest you should say, 'I have made Abram rich'. (Genesis 14:22-23, NKJV)*

Abraham refused to receive anything from Melchizedek, lest Melchizedek would bring up later that he made Abraham the great man that he was.

Abraham knew that if he did things God's way, God would bless him with everything that he needed and more. You are made in the image of God (Genesis 1:26) therefore, as little gods, you can do the same thing that God can do because God lives in you.

Second, the ways to go up in life is to stop doing things that are taking you down. **Jonah's life was a downhill spiral once he disobeyed God;** his life kept going down and down until he decided to come up.

Notice the process of Jonah's downward decline: he went down to Joppa, he saw a ship headed to Tarshish and went down in it, he went down into the sides of the ship, he lay down and went to sleep, he was cast down from the ship, he went down into the sea, he went down into a fish's belly, and there went down to Hell.

This example of Jonah's downward progression should serve as a lesson, indicating today that one of the ways to go up in God is to stop doing what is taking you down or away from God. Only when Jonah made a decision to do things God's way did things start looking up for him, and it is going to be the same way with you; only until you start doing things God's way will things start looking up for you.

Third, you need to know whom you are hanging out with because they can rain on your so-called parade. **Jonah had a negative effect on everybody around**

him, which means that we do not need to be hooking up with just anybody. Jonah was cursed (empowered to fail). It really did not matter what others did to try to make Jonah's situation better, as long as Jonah refused to obey God, the curse on him would remain. The only way the curse could be broken was for Jonah to obey God's instructions.

This is the same way that people are empowered to fail. Jonah, no doubt, was empowered to fail, again and again; he was cursed. The only way Jonah was going to be blessed was by him submitting his will to the will of God. Therefore, it is so important for you to know with whom you are hanging around, because they can either curse you or bless you.

Fourth, God's will for us is to love and forgive all people. **God will use you to be a blessing unto the people who hurt you**. Jonah was a racist; he did not want the city of Nineveh to repent because they did cruel and tortuous things to people. Jonah wanted Nineveh to die and go to Hell but God wanted Nineveh to live, to depart from their evil ways so that He could forgive, love and prosper them.

Notice this passage:

> *When God saw that they had put a stop to their evil ways, He had mercy on them and didn't carry out His threatened destruction.*

This change of plans upset Jonah, and he became very angry. So he complained to the LORD about it: "Didn't I say before I left home that you would do this, LORD? That is why I ran away to Tarshish! I knew that you were a gracious and compassionate God, slow to get angry and filled with unfailing love. I knew easily you could cancel your plans for destroying these people. Just kill me now. LORD! I'd rather be dead than alive because nothing I predicted is going to happen." (Jonah 3:10-4:3, NLT)

God was teaching Jonah and He is teaching us today that it does not matter what people do to you... God expects you to love and forgive them. No matter what people have done to you, you are not responsible for what people do to you; you are responsible for how you **respond** to what people do to you. Your response should always be one of love and forgiveness. Jesus commands us to love our enemy. (Mathew 5:44)

11

Control Yourself

"Why are you so angry?" the Lord asked him. "Why do you look so dejected? You will be accepted if you respond in the right way. But if you refuse to respond correctly, then watch out! Sin is waiting to attack and destroy you, and you must subdue it." (Genesis 4:6–7, NLT)

In the above passage of scripture, God was trying to help Cain stay out of trouble. God's remedy for Cain staying out of trouble was to do the right thing. Rather than doing the right thing, Cain did the wrong thing and he suffered the rest of his life because of a bad decision.

One of the major remedies for breaking a bad habit is just doing what you know you ought to be doing. Do not make excuses, do not procrastinate, do not blame others, but do what you are supposed to do. The bible says in James 4:17 *"Therefore to him that knoweth to do good, and doeth it not, to him it is sin."* The word **good** according to Webster's Dictionary means *to do what is right, proper or correct.*

One of Cain's biggest problems with his brother Abel is that Cain just could not let go of the fact that God had more respect for Abel's offering then his offering. The only thing Cain had to do was to put all of his negative emotions behind him and start doing things right, right meaning the way God wanted him to present his offering. (Genesis 4:3-7)

I find it interesting that Cain struggled to do what is right. It was not that Cain could not do what was right, but he made a decision to hold on to something when he should have let it go. By Cain holding on to dejection, this dejection begins to consume him until he began to have thought of harming his brother, Abel.

These thoughts became so strong until Cain acted out on his bad emotions and it caused him separation from God. (Genesis 4:9-16) The point I want to make in saying all that is this; the only thing Cain had to do in order to get things right with God was to let it go but he refused and suffered the consequences for killing his brother.

With that now said, I personally believe that no one has to tell you that you are doing wrong. I believe that God has put in every human being the ability to discern right from wrong, although, I do believe that some people are better than others at discerning what is right and what is wrong.

Think about this: If a cat knows how to run up a tree for safety when a dog is chasing it, if a fish knows how to swim out of the way when you are cleaning the fish tank, if a bird knows how to fly away if you get too close, why do humans struggle at doing the right thing?

Why does an overeater struggle with eating when he/she knows that he/she should not be eating? What makes an impulsive gambler be willing to lose all of the money, when he/she knows full well that the house payment is due and the baby needs a pair of shoes? How can a person do drugs when he/she knows and is fully consciously aware that doing drugs is going to kill him/her or land him/her in jail or prison?

Why do people smoke cigarettes when they know the label on the back of the carton specifically states that smoking can cause harm, injury or even death? And, yet they still smoke. Why do people do wrong when they know that they should be doing right? I believe one of the reasons is that these people enjoy the sensation of doing the wrong things. Not until they are caught up in the wrong thing and experience so much devastation from the wrong thing, will they want to change and do the right thing.

I think it interesting that when people experience enough headaches and heartaches from doing the wrong thing, their senses come alive. Then, they know what to do and desire to do the right (God) thing. The desire to do the right thing was there in the beginning; it was just that they were so preoccupied with doing the wrong thing that they either did not want to do right, or had no awareness of what was right because they had done wrong for so long.

One way that you can keep the hand of God upon your life and flow in a life of peace and goodness is by making a habit of doing the right thing. When you are undecided on what to do, then do the right thing and you will never go wrong with God. This is what is called character. **Character** is *doing what is right, because it is right.*

This is what King David says in Psalms 51:10 *"Create in me a clean heart, O God; and renew a right spirit within me."* King David knew that the only way to have the favor of God and the blessings of God upon his life was to live right, which would be the result of him doing the right thing.

One of the reasons that people stay bound to things is because they do not take their struggles seriously enough. They hold on to things that they should let go. They do not avoid high-risk situations; they flirt and play around with things they know they should not be doing. This type of behavioral thinking keeps them in bondage and will eventually kill them if they don't gain some type of control over their emotions.

As a chaplain, I observe many sick people in the hospital. In many cases, the illnesses could have been avoided if patients would have done the things that they should have done. Many times, the illness is the result of not carrying out the doctor's orders, abusing the body and waiting until the last stages of the disease. Many people wait until things are way out of control, and then decide that they need to do something.

One reason that bad things happen to good people is that good people get themselves involved in bad things. Then, when bad things are consistently done, the good people make themselves look bad because they are not doing what is good.

Negative situations cannot stop if you are constantly involving yourself in negative activities. The Bible says; *"Be not deceived; God is not mocked: for whatsoever a man soweth, that shall he also reap." (Galatians 6:7)* You receive what you do, whether you want it or not; whatever you sow is exactly what you are going to reap.

12

Manage Your Anger

When you are angry, if you do not let it go, you really end up only hurting yourself. People will not help you nor want to be around you. My wife and I visited a patient in the hospital who was recuperating from an illness for a few days. We were asked by the patient's family to give this patient a visit since the hospital was near our home.

Notice this scripture, *Make no friendship with an angry man; and with a furious man thou shalt not go. Lest thou learn his ways, and get a snare to thy soul. (Proverbs 22:24-25)* No one finds it enjoyable to be around an angry person. After awhile you will want to get away from them.

As we were traveling to the hospital, the Spirit of the Lord told me to go by the bank and get some money to bless this patient. When my wife and I walked into the room, immediately we were unwelcome; the patient who knew us very well was very rude and disrespectful.

The patient who knew my wife extremely well was saying things to my wife that I just did not like. Therefore, after listening approximately five to ten minutes of this person's anger toward us, my wife and I agreed to leave. While going home, I remembered that I forgot to give the person the money that I received from the bank.

I allowed the person's anger to throw me off track. That is precisely what anger will do; it will throw you off track. I did not want to upset the patient; therefore, in a hurry to get out of the room, I forgot to give the patient the money which was intended for her. Anger if misappropriated, will cause hypertension, and distractions; it will throw you off from your intended purpose.

God told me that when people get angry, their blessing passes them by. I wanted to be a blessing to this patient but could not because the patient was mentally hurting too badly to receive it. This patient was so angry, hurt and torn by what they was going through emotionally that the patient's anger caused them not to be helped. Do not run God and people off when you are hurting; be humble and kind to people and they will help you.

> When you are rude and ugly with
> people, you will run people off.

The Bible says, *Make no friendship with an angry man; And with a furious man thou shalt not go: Lest thou learn his ways, And get a snare to thy soul." (Proverbs 22:24-25)* Again, this person was so disrespectful; it wasn't until I had left the hospital that I remembered about the money God told me to give. Anger, improperly managed, causes destruction and confusion. God is not the author of confusion, but peace. (I Corinthians 14:33)

Pointers to Controlling Your Anger

1.) Change Your Environment – Try hanging around people who are calm. When you begin to associate with calm people on a consistent basis, you will learn their ways on how to be calm. Also, pull away from those things that infuriate and make you feel trapped. People become angry when they are doing things they don't like to do; find out what you like to do and do it.

2.) Change how you think – Angry people have a tendency to be very critical and negative. Very seldom do they see or say anything good. Try replacing those critical and negative thoughts with words that are encouraging and inspirational. Start reading material that focuses only on building you up. Share with others those positive things that you have learned from your reading.

3.) Schedule your time appropriately – People often get overwhelmed when they take on more than they can handle. Try scheduling your time to where you are not always in a hurry. When you are constantly in a hurry, you forget things and become upset when people appear to be slowing you down. Manage your time more wisely: If you have a problem with traffic jams, try leaving early or take another route to get to where you need to be comfortably.

4.) Express Yourself – There is nothing wrong with you expressing yourself in an assertive, not aggressive or demanding way. Expressing yourself appropriately is healthy because you get what is in you, out. Thereby, you keep yourself from exploding or expressing mild episodes of anger. When you express yourself, you are preventing pressure from building up in you and giving your anger a way of escape so that you will not blow up.

Often, people fail because they are not confident in God and they are not willing to endure. You can do it determined upon the fact that you are confident in God and that you are willing to endure. *"And let us not be weary in well doing: for in due season we shall reap, if we faint not." (Galatians 6:9)* The Bible gives the solution to making things work, which is faint not.

Simplified, the word **faint** means to *cave-in, give-up, and turn coward to the point of quitting,* however, the word faint does mean much…much more than that. I will explain why in just a moment. Nevertheless, people often desire change to happen right away in their lives and they fail to realize that change, sometimes, will take time.

Change is a process, and in some cases, you will not arrive instantly at your desired level of change. However, in the process of change, it is extremely important to let bad emotions and wrong doings go, and stay focused, disciplined, and do not give up. Again, everything is subject to change except for the word of God.

The word **faint** in its original language (Greek) in Galatians 6:9 is *ekluo* pronounced *ek-loo'-o* which means *to loose or release;* it carries with it the connotation of becoming *to relax.*

I like the original translation of the word faint because it indicates why the person caved in, gave up or turned coward and quit. The reason is that they became too relaxed, which resulted in them caving-in, giving up, turning coward and progressing to the point of quitting.

I shared in my previous book about the story of the rabbit versus the turtle in a race. You would think from a logical perspective that the rabbit would surely win the race because of its speed; however, because the rabbit became overly confident about being so far ahead, it became *too relaxed*. In fact, the rabbit became so relaxed that it went to sleep during the race, thus losing its intended goal.

Esau Madness

Again, another aspect of the word **faint** in its original language is to *release*. When you release something, you turn it over. A good example of this is the story of Esau's birthright. (Genesis 25:29-34):

One day Jacob cooked a pot of stew; Esau, his brother, came in from hunting and was extremely hungry. Esau asked for some stew but his brother refused to give him any unless Esau sold (*released*) his birthright to Jacob. Esau released his birthright signifying that he cared very little for it.

A **birthright** is *an inheritance* – which all the children had a right to share (Luke 15:11-13) – however the portion of the firstborn child's was to be two times bigger than all the other children's inheritance. If there were three children, the inheritance would be divided in four parts. The firstborn child was to receive two parts, and the remaining two children were to receive one part each. (Deuteronomy 21:17)

The point I want to make about Esau is that when he released his birthright this started an avalanche of psychotic behaviors that drove Esau to the point of almost losing his mind. Esau actually thought that Jacob deceived him into selling his birthright, but realistically, Esau chose to release it.

When you allow something to happen in your life, you can not blame others for your irresponsibility.

Notice this scripture,

"Esau replied, "My brother deserves the name Jacob because he has already cheated me twice. The first time he cheated me was out of my right as the first-born son, and now he has cheated me out of my blessing." Then Esau asked his father, "Don't you still have any blessing left for me?" (Genesis 27:36, CEV)

Esau eventually became so mad and angry with his brother Jacob that he wanted to kill him. (Genesis 27:41) Esau felt that Jacob had cheated him twice, but actually, Jacob had only cheated him once, which was out of his father's blessing. For whatever reason, Esau failed to deal with the fact that he sold his birthright to Jacob for a pot of beef stew.

Esau is the responsible party, not Jacob. When Esau sold his birthright, it was no longer stolen because he had turned it over to Jacob. Esau released to Jacob all of the blessings that would be associated with the first-born inheritance. When you allow something to happen in your life, you can not blame others for your irresponsibility.

Apparently, Esau never let the anger go of selling his birthright because later he accuses Jacob of stealing. Again, this lie indicates addictive behavior on Esau's part because he never owns up to his own responsibilities. In addition, if Esau had admitted giving Jacob his birthright, things would have been better inside Esau.

In a nutshell, all of Esau's problems evolved out of the fact that he could not let go of what his brother Jacob had done to him, In addition, he became too relaxed; he released his blessing to his brother. Therefore, because Esau could not handle the fact that he turned over his blessings, he got mad, resulting in him wanting to just cave in, give-up and quit.

I have experienced people who appear to be very successful for a long period, then all of a sudden, they hit bottom. Everything appears to fall apart or go wrong in their lives. I believe that these people became too loose and relaxed; they felt that because they had arrived to success, they did not have to do anything to keep their success.

Notice this scripture: *"Therefore we ought to give the more earnest heed to the things which we have heard, lest at any time we should let them slip." (Hebrews 2:1)* When you start letting things slip and slide by, that is when you set yourself up for a fall; the disappointments of life often occur when you begin to relax. How can an individual know when they are slipping? When you no longer are doing the things that made you successful.

When you faint, you become stagnant; you lose your grip on your focus and start slipping. In boxing terms, you drop your guard. You become too tired or relaxed, which can result in the possibility of a knock out.

The Bible tells us,

> *"be well balanced (temperance, sober of mind), be vigilant and cautious at all times; for that enemy of yours, the devil, roams around like a lion roaring [in fierce hunger], seeking someone to seize upon and devour." (I Peter 5:8, AMP)*

When you faint, you relax until you do not do anything, which opens the door for whatever you are struggling with to come on you and over power (*seizing or devouring*) you to the point of you shutting down, making you have no desire to continue.

The way to overcome when you feel like giving up is to keep doing what you know to do. You have to stay with it; you cannot allow the immediate discomfort or dissatisfaction to cause you to lose heart and quit. Sometimes in life you will just have to ride things out; you just have to stick with it and enjoy the ride, making the best out of a not-so good situation.

13

Don't Come Up Short

An example of not coming up short is when I was at home one night watching a college football game. A defensive back intercepted the football and ran about sixty yards. When he was close to the touch down line he kept looking back; the opposing team player grabbed him by the back of his jersey and pulled him down at the one-yard line.

The point is this: in life, many people keep looking back and because they keep looking back, it slows them down significantly. The looking back prevents them from crossing over or entering into their greatness. Many times, we are right at the point of entering into what we desire but because we turn back or look back, we come up short.

In order to overcome life struggles you have to get it settled that I am going on, no more looking back, or turning back, I forgive myself and I forgive any and everybody who has done me wrong. You have to let things go and not allow yourself to be concerned about what others think, feel, say or do to you. Don't let them stop you from doing what God said you could do.

Notice this scripture, *"And Jesus said unto him, No man, having put his hand to the plough, and looking back, is fit for the kingdom of God." (Luke 9:62)* Basically, what Jesus is communicating is that when you lock hold of the things of God, you cannot have a divided heart. Nothing is to come before the will of God for your life.

Jesus was so emphatic about nothing coming before the will of God, that means no family member, job, circumstance or events was to take precedent over the call of God on one's life. Jesus was requiring a total surrendering to God's leading; you cannot make excuses for not doing the will of God.

Jesus uses the example of plowing and not looking back, this had strong significance to the Jewish community. It was a no-no to plow while looking over your shoulders. You can not plow a perfect row by looking back. For a plowman to look back while he was plowing would make his lines crooked. The field would be much more disorganized and extremely difficult to manage.

One reason why people struggle with the things of God and the blessings of God is because they are compromising the will of God for temporary satisfactions. You will have to deny yourself and obey God, even when it appears to be disrespectful, inconvenient and discomforted. You must understand that God's will is always the best way.

Jesus also uses the word fit. This word **fit** in the Greek is *euthetos,* it means *suitable* or *usable.* When you look back you lose sight of what God is doing, which results in you been disqualified or not suitable to carry out the things of God because you are not in a proper position nor place for God to do what He needs to do.

Jesus was communicating the importance of putting first things first. To be an effective witness for God you will have to have the right priorities. If you are going to successfully complete the will of God for your life, you will have to let some things go, then you will have to put God first in everything and don't look back. (Matthew 6:33)

Works Cited

Buttrick, A. George. *The Interpreters Dictionary of the Bible: An Illustrated Encyclopedia.* Nashville, TN. Abingdon Press. 1962, 2000. P. 547-548.

Colbert, Don. *DEADLY EMOTIONS: UNDER-STANDING THE MIND – BODY – SPIRIT CONNECTION THAT CAN HEAL OR DESTROY YOU.* Nashville, TN. Thomas Nelson, Inc. 2003. P. 169.

Dickow, Gregory. *HOW TO NEVER BE HURT AGAIN.* Chicago, IL. Gregory Dickow Ministries. 2003. P14.

Dollar, Creflo. A. *CLAIM YOUR VICTORY TODAY: 10 Steps That Will Revolutionize Your Life.* New York, NY. Warner Faith. 1993, 2006. P. 19.

_____. *THE COLOR OF LOVE: Understanding God's Answer to Racism, Separation and Division.* Tulsa, Oklahoma. Harrison House, Inc. 1997. P. 8.

_____. *The Hand of God,* (part 2) Teaching on DVD, 10/16/05 at 11:00 am. College Park, Ga, United States of America. 2005.

Hilliard, Bridget. E. *THE WILL TO WIN: Principles for Disciplined Living.* Houston, TX. Light Publications. 2003. P. 9.

King, Martin Luther. Jr. *THE WORDS OF MARTIN LUTHER KING, JR.* New York, NY. Newmarket Press. 1987. P23.

Meyer, Joyce. *Reduce Me To Love.* New York, NY. Time Warner Books, Inc. 2000. P122.

Price, Fredrick K.C. *Faith, Foolishness, or Presumption?* Los Angeles, CA. Faith One Publishing. 1997. P. 97, 99.

_____. *Race, religion, and Racism, Volume One: A Bold Encounter With Division in the Church.* Los Angeles, Ca. Faith One Publishing. 1999. P. 164.

Roberts, Oral. *If You Need HEALING Do These Things.* Tulsa, OK. Oral Roberts Ministries. 2002. P. 45.

About the Author

Loy B. Sweezy, Jr. was born and raised in Shelby, North Carolina. As a child, he attended church on a consistent basis and while there gained a personal intimacy with God. At age 21, he received the Baptism of the Holy Spirit.

Loy B. Sweezy, Jr. is a graduate of East Coast Bible College in Charlotte, North Carolina, with a Bachelor of Science Degree. While at East Coast Bible College, he did missionary work in India, Germany and Jamaica. He is a graduate of the School of Theology in Cleveland, Tennessee, with a Master's Degree. He is currently working on a Doctoral Degree at Oral Roberts University in Tulsa, Oklahoma.

He has worked as a chaplain in pastoral care and counseling department for both Carolina Medical Center in Charlotte, North Carolina and Princeton/Montclair Hospital in Birmingham Alabama. He currently works as a mental health and substance abuse counselor for Ridgeview Institute located in Smyrna, Georgia.

Contact Information

To contact the author write:

Loy Sweezy Ministries
P.O. Box 131
Austell, Georgia 30168

You can order this book and other materials by calling toll-free 1-866-873-6330

Internet Address: **www.loysweezy.com**

Please provide your personal testimony or how this book has helped you when you write. Your prayer requests are welcome.

Books by Loy B. Sweezy, Jr.

Breaking Free

Overcoming Bad Habits

How To Get Out Of A Tough Spot

Notes

Notes

Notes

www.ingramcontent.com/pod-product-compliance
Lightning Source LLC
Chambersburg PA
CBHW051839040426
42447CB00006B/615